The Battle of Kilsyth
15 August 1645

Montrose, Baillie & the Keys to Scotland

HUGH HARKINS

The Battle of Kilsyth
15 August 1645

Montrose, Baillie & the Keys to Scotland

© Hugh Harkins 2018

Centurion Publishing
United Kingdom

ISBN 10: 1-903630-77-0
ISBN 13: 978-1-903630-77-8

This volume first published in 2018

The publisher and author would like to thank all organisations and services for their assistance and contributions in the preparation of this volume

CONTENTS

ABSTRACT

This research paper investigates the battle of Kilsyth, fought on 15 August 1645 between the Scottish Royalist and Scottish Covenanter armies in Scotland commanded by the Marquis of Montrose and General Baillie respectively. Kilsyth was the last in a string of victories for Montrose before, on 13 September 1645, his depleted army was defeated at the battle of Philiphaugh close to Selkirk in the modern day Scottish borders. The paper deals with events leading up to the battle, the battle itself, its effects and its aftermath utilising a number of contemporary reports and government archived papers to detail events leading up to the battle and establish the overall command structure of the Covenanter government and army. In detailing the battle at Kilsyth the paper draws on a number of contemporary accounts – two of which are Baillie's reports to Parliament.

The paper provides an alternative to the conventional view that Montrose, in 1644-1645, conducted a guerilla war against the Scottish Covenanter army in Scotland. The facts, as they were on the ground in 1644-1645, clearly show that for the most part Montrose's army moved as a whole and fought as a whole in a series of pitched battles that earned the Royalist cause a number of major victories in Scotland, culminating with the decisive victory gained at Kilsyth.

As the lay of the land has changed considerably due to human activity in the 373 years that have elapsed since the date of the battle the paper employs a combination of modern topography data, combined with what is known of the areas topography of 1645 and the available contemporary reports of the battlefield to identify the most plausible areas for the dispositions of the opposing armies and the most plausible areas for the various phases of the battle – both areas of current historical debate.

The paper using a basic mathematical process to arrive at values for the rough numbers of troops in each of the opposing armies. With regards to the army of Montrose this is accomplished through an analysis of the best available information of additions and subtractions from his army before the battle of Alford through his threatening parliament at Perth and his retirement to Kilsyth.

Employing documentary evidence, including parliamentary papers, the paper disproves the long held assertion that the Marquis of Argyle was in fact in command of the Covenanter army rather than its documented commander in chief – General Robert Baillie.

The paper answers the question of why in the aftermath of the battle at Kilsyth Montrose did not march on parliament, but instead marched southward to engage the Scottish Covenanter army returning from England and shows that covenanter government in Scotland ceased for many weeks after Montrose's victory at Kilsyth. It also shows that Montrose's defeat at Philiphaugh almost a month after the victory at Kilsyth the catalyst for a Scottish defeat and occupation by English forces half a decade later.

The paper refutes the long held view that Montrose's defeat less than one month after the battle of Kilsyth vastly reduced the battle's importance on the grand scale of the momentous events taking place in the British Isles as the great civil war was drawing to its close. Instead it shows that the victory for Montrose at Kilsyth was a major contributing factor to his ultimate defeat at Philiphaugh the following month. Had Baillie's covenanter army not been destroyed at Kilsyth then the army of Montrose would have been considerably stronger when it met the Scottish covenanter army returning from England as it would have hemorrhaged several thousand highlanders that evidence shows reduced Montrose's army to only about half the strength of his army that fought at Kilsyth.

THE BATTLE OF KILSYTH, 15 AUGUST 1645

Stirling Bridge (September 1297), Falkirk (July 1298), Bannockburn (June 1314), Aberdeen (September 1644), Philiphaugh (September 1645), Prestonpans (September 1745), Culloden Moor (April 1746) – battles in Scottish history, the importance of which has rang down through the historic ages to the present day. A name missing from that list is the little known battle fought on 15 August 1645 at the height of the civil wars, or the 'Wars of the Three Kingdoms', between the English Parliamentarian and Scottish Covenanters on one side and the Royalists on the other. Kilsyth was a small settlement located at the foot the Kilsyth Hills that separated the town from Stirling, a major centre of 1645 Scottish political and military power, which lay some 13 km to the North North East.[1] In terms of importance this battle ranked no less than Falkirk and even the iconic battle that was fought on Culloden Moor on that dreich April day in 1746 when the Jacobite dream of a revival of the Stuart crown was shattered forever. In terms of slaughter, Kilsyth was one of the bloodiest battles in Scottish history. The victory achieved for the Royalist cause at Kilsyth allowed the Marquis of Montrose (James Graham) to occupy Glasgow and, in effect, become the de facto ruler of Scotland, on behalf of the King, Charles I, despite the decision not to march on parliament and install such a government.[2]

It may not be an overstatement to say that Kilsyth qualifies as the forgotten battle, this certainly being true of the battlefield itself. There is certainly a gap in Scottish historiography regarding the battle at Kilsyth, which is universally glossed over as an incidental anecdote to the wider civil war gripping the British Isles in 1645. This situation stems from the battle and its immediate repercussion, to a large extent, being largely ignored by the more than three and a half centuries of historiography. There are no museums to the battle as can be found for

---

[1] The Kilsyth Hills are an easterly continuation of the Campsie Fells range

[2] Charles I acceded to the throne in 1625 on the death of James VI (Scotland)/James I (England), continuing the Stuart monarchy

Bannockburn or Culloden, and only a small memorial close to the site of the battle marks the event. Aiding Kilsyth's immersion into the black hole of historiography is the fact that there is little discernable battlefield for the modern day archeologist to excavate (there has been no archeological excavation at the site), a major portion of the site having been developed into a man-made canal-feeder reservoir in the late eighteenth century under the grand project that spawned the Forth and Clyde Canal.[3]

BACKGROUND

The battle of Kilsyth was fought between the Royalist forces under the 1st Marquis of Montrose and the Scottish Covenanter army under General Robert Baillie during the civil wars that had engulfed the British Isles in the 1640's. One could fill an entire volume with the reasons for and major events leading to the civil wars and still be left open to criticism for leaving important events out. However, for the purposes of this paper space dictates that a very brief background leading to the events of 1644-1645 should suffice, starting with the accession of Charles I who, following the death of James VI (Scotland)/James I (England), inherited the thrones of Scotland, England and Ireland in 1625. In the same period, England had joined Protestant Union and Charles I was married to Henrietta Maria, the Catholic daughter of the king of France, Henry IV. In England, Charles I entered into a period of direct rule without resort to parliament in 1629, this lasting into 1640, a period of eleven years. In 1633, during this period of direct rule in England, Charles I had his coronation at Edinburgh, Scotland, in which year the Scottish Parliament met, and, in 1636, the list of new cannons for the Church of Scotland was published, followed the following year by the publication of a new book of liturgy (prayer book) for the Church of Scotland. This was considered a provocation to much of the populace, leading to a riot, in direct protest at publication of the new prayer book, at St Giles Cathedral in Edinburgh on 23 July 1637. In 1638, the National Covenant was signed for Scotland and Charles I had to agree to withdrawal of the new prayer book that had incited the riot the previous year.[4] There followed the 'First Bishops War' of May-June 1639, which was brought to a close with the pacification of the town of Berwick. In this year the episcopacy was abolished in Scotland. The 'Second Bishop's War' of August-October 1640 was brought to a close by the treaty of Ripon in October that year. The year 1640 also saw the meeting of the Short Parliament in England (April) as Charles I's period of direct rule ended. This parliament was

---

[3] Building work on the Forth & Clyde canal commenced in June 1768 and the canal, stretching from the Firth of Forth in the East of Scotland to the Firth of Clyde in the West, was officially opened in summer 1790 (Forth & Clyde Canal Society). We know very little about the canal-feeder reservoir site, other than that it was a natural glen, prior to its development as Townhead reservoir (now named Banton Loch) between first survey in 1770 and being filled to capacity with around 750,000 m³ of water in 1773

[4] The National Covenant, signed at Greyfriars kirk in Edinburgh, was in effect a contract with God designed to ensure the purity of the Scottish kirk

dissolved in May 1640, followed by a meeting of the Long Parliament in November that year. The following year the Triennial Act was passed in England and Wales, and, in July 1641, an Act that abolished prerogative courts of the Star Chamber and High Commission, followed by what became known as the Grand remonstrance in protest in December 1641 (OU A200).

The year 1642 was when the conflict known as the First Civil War (1642-1646) began in England with the Parliamentarians opposed to the Royalists under Charles I, the standard of the latter being raised at Nottingham on 22 August that year as a prelude to the Battle of Edgehill on 23 October 1642 – the first major engagement between Parliamentarian and Royalist forces in the first civil war, a victory being gained by the latter.[5] In June the following year, the Westminster Assembly of Divines was put in place, representation from Scotland joining in August that year. This was followed by the act of the Solemn League and Covenant of September 1643 in which the Scottish Covenanter parliament pledged to send a Scottish army to England to help the Parliamentarian war effort against the Royalist army (OU A200). This deepening political alienation for the Royalist cause in Scotland and the war preparations by the Scottish Covenants resulted in Charles I recruiting, as allies, the Scottish and Irish Gaels, which he had previously treated with contempt. Scottish clan support for both causes – Royalist and Covenanter – fluctuated during the war. For example, devastation reaped on some highland Clan lands by Covenanter forces in the winter of 1644 was a driver for six clans to switch to the Royalist cause (Harris & McDonald, 2007a).

There is historical debate over the reason(s) for Scottish Gaels supporting Charles I. Whilst the Covenanters were militarily pressing demands against the Highland clans, the major reason for Gaels allying with Charles may have been a McDonnell plan to bring Irish Gaels to join with Clan Donald in a campaign against the Campbell's to recover lost lands.[6] The Macdonald clan had been a powerful influence in Scotland, controlling lands in the Western Isles, Kintyre, Knapdale, Lochabar, Ardnamurchan, Morvern and the earldom of Ross (Harris & MacDonald, 2007). After the forfeiture of the Lordship of the Isles in 1493, the McDonald clan (Clan Donald) fortunes rapidly spiraled downwards. The so called 'fire and sword' policy saw the crown commissioning one clan to police others, the Campbell's being in the kings favour at the expense of the McDonald's (Harris & MacDonald, 2007a). Whatever the reasoning for the Gael's joining Charles cause, the new alliance proved of fundamental importance to the Royalist campaign. In this respect it can be argued that some clans were violently opposing the central government in Edinburgh (Covenanter parliament), but, on the other hand, they were supporting the crown (21 of 47 main clans supported the crown) in the Scottish dimension of the civil wars

---

[5] The outcome of this battle is courted in controversy, but it must be concluded that it was a victory for the Royalist cause as the Parliamentarian army, intending to prevent the Royalist army from being able to make use of the road to London, was forced to withdraw northward to seek safety from the garrisons of Warwick and Coventry, leaving control of the road to London in Royalist hands

[6] The Campbell's were a major part of the Scottish power base in Covenanter Scotland

gripping the British Isles. There is no doubting that the availability of men from the Highland clans was crucial to Montrose's ability to successfully wage war on the Covenanter's. Regardless of the reason for some of the clans joining the Royalist cause, religious issues other than opposing the Campbell's being but one of those put forward, Gael armed rebellion in opposition to the central government is considered lawlessness by the clans by some historians. However, this is a fallacious view. The Highland clams joining Montrose should not be viewed as the 'lawless' Highlanders rallying to a fight due to a low threshold for the resort to violence as has often been portrayed (Harris & MacDonald, 2007). In reality, from the late sixteenth century, major inter clan fighting had declined significantly, the lawless label attached to the clans being, perhaps, undeserved. Supporting this assertion is the argument that the Scottish governments viewed the Highlands as having been largely 'pacified' from 1616 and that small scale outbreaks of violence in 1617 and 1620 were the exception rather than the rule (Lynch, 2000).

The Highland clans are equally often portrayed as undisciplined barbarians, but the contrary may actually have been the case in regard to many clans, certainly for the early modern period that covered the 1640's. Scottish clan society, thought to have appeared in the eleventh and twelfth centuries, was effectively, but not exclusively, a society of kinship of the indigenous populations, this being known as feudal society. This Gaelic society was distinct form the Lowland Scottish society and the society of Irish Gaels (Harris & MacDonald, 2007). The clan armies, in fact, consisted, for the most part, of disciplined warriors acting at the behest of the clan chief. Despite the Scottish clans, together with the sizeable contingent of Irish Gaels, making up the lion's share of Montrose's forces, the army should be viewed in the context of a Scottish Royalist army rather than as a hoard of Highland barbarians descending on the Lowlands. Three regiments of Irish Gaels served in the Scottish Royalist army in Scotland during the 1644-1645 campaign. The Irish Gaels, under the command of Alasdair MacColla (McColla), joined forces with Montrose, the overall commander of the combined Royalist force in Scotland, in August 1644. The Irish Gaels were considered to have been professional disciplined troops and brought considerable fighting value to the ranks of Montrose's makeshift army (Harris & MacDonald, 2007a).

The campaign of Montrose in 1644-1645 is almost universally described as a guerrilla war conducted against the superior, in numbers, forces of the Scottish Covenanters. However, in actuality, Montrose's army moved as a whole and fought as a whole in a series of pitched battles that earned the Royalist cause a number of major victories in Scotland that culminated with the decisive victory gained at Kilsyth. The fallacious idea that Montrose was conducting a guerrilla war has emerged over the centuries due, at least in part, to the fact that his army failed to capture and garrison large towns. However, to provide such garrisons would have been to split the army piecemeal and put Montrose on the defensive rather than the offensive, which would have been detrimental to the war aims – defeat the Scottish Covenanter army(s) in Scotland and advance on England to engage the Scottish Covenanter army in England should it not return to Scotland to face the threat in its rear.

A Scottish army had been dispatched to England under the terms of the Act of Solemn League and Covenant of 1643, in which the Scottish parliament endeavored to send a Scottish army to England in September that year to support the parliamentarian cause against the Royalist army (OU A200). The dispatch of this army was a serious blow to the Royalist cause, causing consternation among those supporters of the Royalist cause in Scotland.

It would be prudent to recount the major incidents of the Civil War in Scotland during the course of 1644 and leading up to the battle at Kilsyth in August 1645. Montrose had taken up the banner of the Royalist cause in Scotland after the Covenanting government had come down on the Parliamentarian side in the Civil War in England, which pitted the Parliamentarians against the Royalists under Charles I.[7] Having raised a modest force of 2,000-3,000 men, Montrose, at the Battle of Tippermuir on 1 September 1644, won a victory against a Covenanter army led by Lord Elcho.[8] The Covenanters suffered considerable losses that have been estimated at between 1,000 and 2,000 men, for very small loss on the Royalist side. The next major engagement of the campaign saw a force of around 3,000 Covenanters, under the command of Lord Burleigh, defeated, by a Royalist force estimated at about half the Covenanter number, commanded by Montrose, at the Battle of Aberdeen on 13 September 1644. Losses were again severe for the Covenanters as they fled the field to seek sanctuary in the town of Aberdeen – losses on the Royalist side again being recorded as meagre. The next major engagement was at the battle of Inverlochy on 2 February 1645.[9] This resulted in another Royalist victory when Montrose's force of around 1,500 men defeated a Covenanter army, estimated at around 3,000 in number, under the command of Sir John Hurry, with the Marquis of Argyle in Company.[10] The Covenanter army lost an estimated 1,500-1,700 men.

~~The next major battle betw~~een the Covenanter and Royalist armies took place at

[7] In basic terms the English Parliamentarians wanted a constitutional monarchy with recourse to later abolish it altogether, while the Royalist's favoured monarchic rule. In Scotland, it was somewhat more complicated as Charles I had not just emerged from a period of direct rule as he had in England. In this respect, Charles I had not enjoyed the same power in Scotland as he had in England and the Royalist army was primarily focussed on removing or diminishing Covenanter rule in that country

[8] Tippermuir is in the locality of Perth. The covenanter army is often stated as in excess of 6,500 strong, but was probably somewhat smaller than this in overall numbers and considerably smaller if only trained men of arms are considered

[9] Inverlochy lies just North of Fort William on the western edge of the Ben Nevis mountain range

[10] This Covenanter force is thought to have contained a sizeable contingent of the Campbell's in company with Archibald Campbell, the Marquis of Argyle whom, it is stated in some accounts, left the field and sought safety on a ship moored in Loch Linnhe, which commences its northern part a few miles west of Glencoe, just over 10 km on a line southward of Fort William

Auldearn on 9 May 1645.[11] This resulted in another victory for Montrose's army, which defeated a much larger force of Covenanters. The last major engagement between Covenanter and Royalist forces before the two armies met at Kilsyth took place at Alford on 2 July 1645.[12] The Royalist army achieved yet another victory over the Covenanters with estimates of 1,500 killed on the Covenanter side. A prudent estimate for the number killed on the Royalist side would be in the region of 400. However, while Montrose had achieved considerable success in Scotland, the overall Royalist cause suffered a disastrous setback when Charles I was defeated by an English Parliamentarians army at Naseby, England, on 14 June 1645. This left the Royalist army in Scotland as being the major hope for Charles I's cause.

It would also be prudent to recount the movements of the various armies well in advance of the battle at Kilsyth in order to get a better idea of the composition of the opposing forces at Kilsyth, in particular that of Montrose's army, which has hitherto been based mostly on conjecture. While in the vicinity of Loch Katrine, just as spring was turning to summer 1645, Montrose was informed that a strong Covenanter force, commanded by Sir John Hurry, was moving against Lord Gordon who was positioned in the area of Auchindoun.[13] He was also informed that General Robert Baillie was laying waste to Athol and threatening Montrose's supplies located at Blair Athol Castle.[14] Montrose rapidly moved his army, in its entirety, northerly to meet the threat that was Hurry in the Grampians.[15] Around 1 May 1645, Lord Gordon rejoined Montrose's army on the River Dee, increasing Montrose's strength

[11] Auldearn lies somewhat over 20 km North eastward from Inverness

[12] Alford lies in excess of 35 km on a line North westerly of Aberdeen

[13] Lock Katrine lies on the North side of the Trossachs mountain range and around 6 km North East of Ben Lomond in the West of Scotland. Auchindoun lies somewhat under 60 km easterly of Inverness

[14] Blair Athol Castle lies about 40 km North westerly of Perth

[15] The Grampians mountain range lies to the southward of the Cairngorms mountain range about 60 km or so, depending on location within the Grampians, southward of Inverness

[16] The River Dee, which enters the North Sea at Aberdeen, rises from the Cairngorms mountain range

[17] The River Spey, which rises at Loch Spey to the South East of the Cairngorms, runs its course North westward of the River Dee

[18] Baillie's campaign in Athol had compelled the release from Montrose's army of an undetermined number of those men from that area to return home, although many highlanders remained with the army along with the Irish under MacColla (Napier, c1838)

[19] We hear from Baillie that all of the 1200 foot Hurry had taken into Inverness had been lost at Auldearn (Napier, c1838). Royalist casualties at Auldearn were reported as about 20 killed and about 200 wounded (Napier, c1838)

by 1,000 foot troops and some 200 horse troops.[16] The Royalist army strength was further increased when Macdonald rejoined with a highland division (probably regimental strength). Hurry, on hearing of Montrose's proximity, withdrew his army across the River Spey.[17] When at Inverness Hurry joined with troops from the northern Covenanter forces, consisting of the Frazer's and troops from Moray and Caithness. Hurry was pursued by Montrose until the halt at Auldearn. At this point Montrose's strength was estimated at 2,000-3,000, foot and horse troops, and he decided to avoid battle if possible[18] (Napier, c1838). However, emboldened by his superior, in numbers, force, Hurry decided to take battle to Montrose. Informed that Baillie was advancing on the Spey, Montrose risked being trapped between two armies, each of superior strength to his own. It was thus decided to accept battle with Hurry at Auldearn, resulting in a decisive victory for the Royalist cause[19]. This left no effective Covenanter military force in the North of the country.[20] There was still the army of Baillie to consider and, in the second half of May 1645, this was positioned to threaten Montrose's army, which had already re-crossed the Spey. Baillie's army, which was already superior in horse troops to that of Montrose, had been reinforced, when camped in a forest at Cochlarochie, by the remnants of Hurry's horse troops that had escaped at Auldearn – about 100 or so (Napier, c1838). It is also thought that Baillie's army was superior to Montrose in foot troops, although there is certainly uncertainty in this regard. Ballie, being urged by the Committee of Estates to force a situation that would lead to battle, expected Montrose to give just that despite the unfavorable conditions faced by the Royalist army. Montrose, however, decided not to give battle until his army was strengthened and the scene was actually being set for Montrose's retirement with Baillie in pursuit. During the first phase of the pursuit Baillie got close to the Royalist army, apparently just over six miles separating the two armies in the area of Glenlivet, South East of the River Spey on the northern edge of what is the modern day Cairngorms National Park and they were within sight of each other at Badenoch.[21] Montrose, although declining full scale battle, harassed Baillie's army, which, through lack of provisions, was forced to withdraw North to Inverness.[22] This left Montrose to continue the move of his army southward, where a new threat was emerging as Ludovic Lindsay, the 16th Earl of Crawford, had taken the field with a new Covenanter army, no doubt hoping to make a name for himself by succeeding where Argyle, Hurry and Baillie

[20] Some sources state that in victory Montrose showed similar cruelties to that of the Covenanters by laying waste to the estates of those Royalist held responsible for previous atrocities (Napier, c1838)

[21] Glenlivet is some 40 km South East of Inverness. Badenoch lies around 1-2 km south west of Aviemore on the western edge of the cairngorms

[22] Baillie's letters state only that the withdrawal of the Covenanter army to Inverness was for want of food, but other sources, particularly Napier, c1838, suggest that this was a withdrawal in panic brought on by harassment tactics and skirmishes initiated by the Royalist army. However, while it is accepted that such actions took place, it is doubtful that this was the reason for Baillie's withdrawal, considering he, at the behest of the Committee of Estates, was seeking to bring the Royalist army to battle

had failed.[23] Montrose now moved his army quickly across the Grampian mountain range with the intention of destroying Lindsay's new untrained army before any junction could be made with Baillie in the North. Montrose's army arrived at the River Airlie, unbeknownst to Lindsay only some seven miles distant. The scene seemed set for the destruction of Lindsay's army, but Aboyne and most of Montrose's northern troops left the Royalist army to return home[24] (Napier, c1838). The plan to attack Lindsay was abandoned as Montrose took his much depleted army North to the Castle at Corgarth (Corgarff) while Macdonald was sent to the North of Scotland to recruit more forces to replenish the ranks.[25] In this respect, Lord Gordon, in company with Nathanial Gordon, was dispatched to try to bring back some of those northerners that had left the ranks of the army (Napier, c1838).

Lindsay, although not joining with Baillie, apparently revived around 1,000 experienced troops from the formers army in exchange for around 1,000 inexperienced foot troops, although definitive confirmation of this exchange is not available. Lindsay then went on a campaign that ravaged Athol, while Baillie ravaged northern lands associated with nobbles in Montrose's army. Baillie's actions resulted in Montrose again taking his army, reinforced by the return of Aboyne and some of the Gordon horse troops, northward to seek a battle with Baillie's army, which, as noted above, eventually took place at Alford Hill on 2 July 1645 when Montrose gained yet another victory over the Covenanter armies in Scotland[26] (Napier, c1838). The victory at Alford opened up the possibility for Montrose to march on Parliament, which was in upheaval due to pestilence.[27] Parliament sat at Stirling on 8 July 1645. It is on this day the act was passed for raising a new army to put before Montrose (Napier, c1838). As pestilence was now present in Stirling Parliament moved again, this time to Perth, where it sat on 24 July and again on 30 July[28] (Napier, c1838). On hearing that Parliament was sitting at Perth Montrose endeavoured to advance on that town and spread confusion and, if possible, cause

[23] Montrose and Lindsay (the Earl of Crawford) were well acquainted and had apparently even discussed what they referred to as the form of dictatorship rule of the Marquis of Argyle. Lindsay had also apparently been critical of the Marquis of Argyle's military campaigns

[24] Aboyne left Montrose under the reason of going to Strathbogie as he was invalided, but this is considered a pretext by some, although there is no credible evidence to support the pretext theory. Lord Gordon remained with Montrose, although many Gordons left the army and returned home

[25] Corgarff Castle is located about 50 km westward of Aberdeen

[26] The opposing forces at Alford were relatively even in foot troops – about 2,000 each, but Baillie had the advantage in horse troops – around 600 compared with Montrose's 250 or so (Napier, c1838)

[27] Parliament had relocated from Edinburgh to Stirling thence to Perth as the presence of bubonic plague in Edinburgh had forced it to flee that town in May 1645 and not return until March 1646 (Volume 18, GSC 1637-1651, XXXI & 1, 1982

[28] Perth had been selected as this was one of the assembly areas for the new army, which it was hoped, could reach a strength of 8,000-10,000 foot troops and perhaps 500 horse troops

parliament to take flight.

MONTROSE THREATENS AND THEN RETIRES FROM PERTH

Montrose's horse troops, which were depleted following the battle of Alford, were estimated at around 100 only as he planned his next moves. While the situation was far from satisfactory in regards to horse, foot troops were considered to be in good condition and further reinforcements were expected from the Earl of Aboyne and the Earl of Airlie (The History of the Scottish Wars, 1825). Montrose moved to Angus where his army was strengthened by the addition of troops from Athol. Macdonald also rejoined Montrose at Angus, bringing with him 700 of the Maclean Highlanders with Maclean at their head, 500 Clanranald with the Captain of Clanranald at their head, Glengarry with another 500 and smaller numbers from the McGregor's, Macnabs (both headed by their clan chiefs) and some Macphersons and Farquharsons. This considerable body of reinforcements brought Montrose's army to around 4,000-5,000 strong (Napier, c1838). Montrose was apparently expecting the Earl of Huntley with a considerable body of men from the Gordon's, but was dismayed when he did not arrive, only 100 or horse troops being provided, though welcome they must have been considering Montrose was poor in cavalry.

Some historians put the overall number of troops now with Montrose at around 6,000. However, this value is reached by adding the numbers that Montrose possessed at Auldearn to the numbers of Highlanders that joined the standard at Angus. It also takes into account perhaps 1200 foot and 300 horse troops later provided by Aboyne and the Earl of Airlie, not available to Montrose as he threatened Perth.[29] It fails to take into consideration the natural wastage through those leaving the ranks after Auldearn.[30] We have to accept that in the absence of complete records the true number of troops on either side in the battles, be it Auldearn, Alford or, Kilsyth, will never be known.

Although the reinforcements he had received swelled the ranks of Montrose's army it was still considerably outnumbered by the Covenanter forces arrayed against him in the vicinity of Perth. It was estimated that this army stood at 6,000 strong, not including the covenanter garrison in Perth itself, to which could be added another 400 or so horse allocated for the protection of Parliament, then residing in that town (Napier, c1838). Despite his disadvantage in numbers Montrose crossed the River Tay and moved toward Perth as he still hoped to be joined by the rest of Aboyne's cavalry.[31] Toward the end of July 1645 Montrose's army was positioned in a forest at Methven westward of Perth.[32] Montrose, considering his army not strong enough for

---

[29] The Earl of Airlie joined Montrose in the area of Dunkeld just before the main royalist retirement and covenanter pursuit to the South of the River Forth, which ended with the battle at Kilsyth

[30] See footnote 18

[31] The River Tay has its rise at a spring on Ben Lui, but is really referred to as the Tay only after passing through Loch Tay. The river snakes North (around 15 km) and East of Perth.

a direct assault on Perth and wishing to avoid a large Covenanter force appearing from that direction, mounted a faint operation in that his cavalry, augmented by 100 or so Musketeers mounted on horses from the baggage train, maneuvered outside Perth. This caused panic that led to the gates of the town being closed, the garrison remaining within for a time. However, the initial panic within the Covenanter command was soon arrested as it became clear that Montrose was poor in cavalry, evinced by his decision not to attack Perth directly, but to go around with a hold on local high ground. Once it became clear that Montrose's operation was little more than a demonstration the Covenanter army, which had been reinforced by forces from outlying areas, including within Fife (The History of the Scottish Wars, 1825) were emboldened by their superior numbers and came forth with the intent to give battle (Napier, c1838). Montrose now chose to withdraw and so began the Covenanter army pursuit of the Royalist army which would end, following various twists and turns, with the battle at Kilsyth on 15 August 1645.[33]

Aboyne, in company with Colonel Nathaniel Gordon, joined with Montrose in the area of Dunkeld.[34] Aboyne and Gordon brought only scant reinforcements in the shape of around 200 cavalry and just over 100 Musketeers, the latter mounted on horses from the baggage train. The Earl of Airlie, having recovered from illness, also joined with Montrose at this time, bringing with him some eighty mounted men of the Ogilvy's, including the Earl's son, Sir David Ogilvy (The History of the Scottish Wars, 1825 &Napier, c1838).

Montrose's retirement from Perth can in no way be described as flight. He maneuvered his army skillfully using asymmetric means to repulse a number of Covenanter attacks on his rear columns. Turning on their pursuers, Montrose's army chased the Covenanter's out of Methven forest, but as the latter would not give full-scale battle, the game of maneuver and counter manoeuvre between the two armies continued (Napier, c1838). There is some question as to whether or not Montrose intended to give battle to the Covenanter army at this time as he was aware of the fact that the Covenanters occupied a strong defensive position (The History of the Scottish Wars, 1825). Montrose continued his withdrawal, the Covenanters again taking up the pursuit, which took the opposing forces into Fife, a Covenanter stronghold. The strength of the Covenanters in Fife brought Montrose to the decision that it would be folly to advance farther than Kinross. He therefore wheeled in the direction of Stirling on the south side of the River Forth (The History of the Scottish Wars, 1825). By moving South and crossing the Forth Montrose would have

[32] Methven lies about 4-5 km west of Perth and about 15-18 km southward of the River Tay near Dunkeld. Dunkeld lies just North of the River Tay on a line some 15-20 or so km North westerly of Perth

[33] This was not a straight forward withdrawal and pursuit. At times the roles were reversed as Montrose manoeuvred his army to threaten the Covenanter army

[34] Aboyne, in company with Colonel Nathaniel Gordon, is stated to have joined with Montrose in the area of Dunkeld, but, considering Montrose's dispositions were near Methven, this junction may well have taken place further southward

been in a position to exert control over the South of Scotland should the main Covenanter army remain to the North of the Forth (Napier, c1838).

MONTROSE MOVES FROM ALLOA TO KILSYTH VIA STIRLING WITH BAILLIE IN PURSUIT

Under Montrose's orders, Macdonald moved westward with the foot troops while Montrose moved to Alloa with much of the horse troops.[35] On hearing of the approach of covenanter forces Montrose departed Alloa with haste and moved to put himself in an overtake position of his foot troops (Napier, c1838). In the vicinity of Stirling Montrose received news that the Covenanter army, under the overall command of General Robert Baillie, was preparing to offer battle. He was also informed of the raising of further forces for the covenanters and the raising of revenue through levies for the covenanter war effort raided by the Earls of Lanark, Englinton, Cassiles, Glengairn and other areas. Although the Covenanter army was superior in numbers to that of Montrose, by the time the former approached Stirling the Royalist army was larger and more experienced than it had been at any point since its formation the previous year. As well as around 5,000 foot soldiers Montrose's horse troops, which had been further replenished, now numbered about 500 (The History of the Scottish Wars, 1825).

Montrose took the decision not to move on Stirling as this town had been struck by pestilence and he lacked the resources or, indeed, the time for a siege of the castle located there and Covenanter forces were in close pursuit. Montrose ordered his army to cross the rivers Forth and Teith some two miles North of Stirling (the Teith joins the Forth around this juncture) from where it was intended to March to Kilsyth, around 18 km across the Kilsyth Hills.[36] The Royalist army crossed the River Carron at Carron Bridge (Napier, c1838) laying in the Carron Valley about 6-7 km North East of Kilsyth.[37] Today there are few, if any areas, of the River Carron that would prevent a person, willing to get their legs wet, from crossing. It is often implied that Montrose had to cross the Carron at Carron Bridge, but the convenience of the Bridge was brought about not by a necessity that this was the only way across, but that it was on the direct route across the hills to Montrose's destination, Kilsyth.[38] Having crossed at Carron Bridge it was around a four or so

[35] Alloa lies on the North Shore of the River Forth about 5 km East of Stirling

[36] The Kilsyth Hills are an eastward extension of the Campsie Fells range with an average height of 900 ft. ± 100 ft. above Kilsyth

[37] Today the River Carron proper commences from Carron Valley Reservoir (Carron Valley runs through the Campsie Feels along its line). In 1645, the rise of the River Carron would have commenced from the small burns in the region of the highest feature of the Campsie Fells, the Meikle Bin, which has a summit at an elevation in the region of 400 m 1,312 ft. in 2018) – Bin Burn and, perhaps, Braes Burn, emptying into a boggy valley (the current location of Carron Valley Reservoir, which was developed much later) four or so km from Carron Bridge where Montrose's army crossed the river

mile march along the ups and downs and twists and turns of the Tak Ma Doon Road that led, as it does in the modern day, into the town of Kilsyth located in the Kelvin Valley.

TOPOGRAPHY OF THE AREA OF KILSYTH

The source Napier (c1838) suggests that Montrose decided to wait at Kilsyth and offer battle to the Covenanting army as the ground was found to be very suitable for defence (Napier, c1838). In respect of a force defending against an army advancing from an eastward direction this would certainly be true. Dullatur bog lay several hundred metres to the southward whilst the rising ground to the North (the lower slopes of the Kilsyth Hills) would prove problematic to any army attempting to outflank the defenders. To bypass the Dullatur bog would have required a march over the hilly ground to the South of the bog, a natural indigenous forest that covers much of this today may well have existed in 1645.[39] This would have taken the army a mile or so South where, after a short westward movement, it would have been possible to cut through a sloping valley, heading almost North directly toward Kilsyth with Dullatur bog to the East and Bar Hill to the West (the hill to the South of Dullatur bog is known as Croy Hill. This and Bar Hill were adjoined by a common link in that the Antoine Wall cut through both.[40]

While human developments have effectively removed Dullatur bog from the landscape (the Forth and Clyde canal now runs through the area that was bog land), the area remains very soft and prone to flooding in the modern age (much of the areas is now rather soggy pastureland for horses), but would still be relatively easily traversable for a person on foot and would present few problems to horse-borne personnel. However, 373 years ago the bog would have presented a formidable obstacle to an army attempting to traverse it, many areas being deep enough for a person or horse to sink completely below the surface.

The glen that runs northward from an area that slopes westward to the village of Croy is flanked by the uplands leading down toward Dullatur bog on the right and the upland eastern slope of Bar Hill on the left. As flood plain and bog land run along most of Kilsyth's southern boundary, even in 2018, it is reasonable to conclude that the lower extension of this area, just before entering Kilsyth, was bog land in 1645, with a developed pathway for carts leading from the village of Croy to the South East of Kilsyth down into Kilsyth proper, a crossing of the River Kelvin (only four or so metres wide, and less in many areas) having to be conducted over a suitable bridge. The River Kelvin runs along the southern boundary of modern day

[38] While the water depth may not have presented a formidable obstacle to the foot or horse troops, the baggage train would have been reliant on the bridge

[39] The term indigenous forest is used to denote a natural forest rather than the many human induced forests planted centuries later to sustain timber requirements

[40] The Antoine Wall, which stretches from the Clyde in the West to the Forth in the East, was built by the Romans, effectively marking the northern limit of their conquest of Britain

Kilsyth and continues toward the soggy area to the East of Kilsyth that separates Kilsyth and Dullatur to the South East of Kilsyth. Today this river is only deep enough to present problems in fording when the water rises after significant rainfall for some days. While we know the weather in Kilsyth was dry and very warm on 15 August 1645, there is no accurate way to determine the areas rainfall in the days or weeks before that fateful day as this period preceded the introduction of rainfall record keeping. However, despite its narrow width, in the Kilsyth area much of the River Kelvin would present problems for horses and horse drawn transport such as carts, due to the steep banks that can average a metre high in places and extend to more than two metres in others. There is no way to be certain of what height or inclination the banks of the Kelvin were in the Kilsyth area in 1645. It has to be concluded that an attack on Kilsyth from the southerly direction would have been as disadvantageous to an attacker as an attack from easterly, with Dullatur bog to the South and the hilly ground of the Kilsyth Hills to the North. Furthermore, at the bottom of the downward slope, just before entering Kilsyth, the ground rose considerably, affording any defenders an overlooking position against an attacking force.

If an attacking army had continued westward instead of entering the glen in a northward direction toward Kilsyth, then it would have bypassed Bar Hill, and, after crossing some boggy ground, would have been able to advance on Kilsyth from the westward only to encounter similar conditions that confronted an army advancing from the eastward direction – steeply rising ground of the Kilsyth Hills to the North and the bog land to the South that still exists to an extent in 2018, with the River Kelvin, Garrel Burn and the burn of Dock Water, which runs into the River Kelvin, running through its length.

The decision by Montrose to wait at Kilsyth and invite the Covenanter army to give battle was brought about by a number of factors. There is no doubt that the terrain, uninviting to an attacking army, was a major point. However, the decision was not based on this alone. Already with the knowledge that the Covenanter Army under Baillie was closing on Kilsyth on a route that circumvented the Kilsyth Hills, Montrose also had to consider that as well as news that a Covenanter force was being raised by Cassilis, Eglinton and Glencairn in the West of Scotland to reinforce Baillie's Covenanter army, a Covenanter force, stated as large, but with no numbers indicated, was being raised in the Clydesdale area to oppose Montrose in case of an advance on Glasgow by the latter (Napier, c1838). This force, which would have been of questionable fighting efficiency, would, at the time Montrose arrived at Kilsyth, have been located around 15 miles South westerly had it been assembled. Despite its questionable fighting value, to depart Kilsyth, with Baillie continuing the pursuit, Montrose faced the prospect of being caught between two Covenanter armies, which would possess an even larger advantage in numbers than that possessed by Baillie's army closing from the North East. To fight and defeat Baillie's army would remove the threat to Montrose from the lesser Covenanting forces in the West and South West, which would be faced with the choices of melting away, disbanding completely or destruction at the hands of Montrose's superior army.

THE ISSUE OF COMMAND OF THE COVENANTER ARMY

Before detailing Baillie's move to Kilsyth, the opposing forces and the battle itself, an area of utmost importance that must be addressed is that of the command of the Covenanter army at Kilsyth. This has been a major point of contention over the centuries, with sources such as Napier (c1838) suggesting that, although General Baillie was at the armies head, the Marquis of Argyle was, in actuality, in command of that army. This assertion, which has continued into the 21st century, probably stems from statements that may have been viewed as Ballie's own contradiction of his own assertion that he was in full command as he indicated that Argyle took control at points, stating:

"While I was present, others did sometimes undertake the command of the army; without either my order or knowledge, fire was raised, and that destroyed which might have been a recompense to some good deserver, for which I would not be answerable to the public" (Napier, c1838).

Whilst Baillie produced such language as evidence (the source Napier (c1838) does not identify the source of this statement) to absolve himself of reasonability for the defeat at Kilsyth, such a statement, if authentic, would merely serve to demonstrate inefficiency as an army commander, or at least his inability exercise his authority over those under his command.[41] It in no way evinces that he was not in command of the army. On the contrary, it is a further statement of his position as commander of the army.

Initially it was expected that the Marquis of Argyll would be in overall command of the forces opposed to Montrose. However, this was not to be. One reason suggested is that Argyll refused the commission to lead the army against Montrose, which is why General Baillie was called on to travel North from England.[42] If there is truth in this then it leaves open to speculation the reason why Argyle refused command, the most compelling hypothesis being that Argyle considered his authority would be damaged in the event of a catastrophic defeat at the hands of Montrose. To be a subordinate commander of a defeated army would be less damning than if he were commander in chief. That said, it is widely considered that General Baillie was summoned North simply as a figurehead for the army and that the Marquis of Argyle would lead in all but name (Napier, c1838), this assumption continuing through the centuries, distorting the facts along the way.

General Baillie states that on his arrival in Scotland he found he could not get either the Marquis of Argyle or the Earl of Lothian to 'continue their employment against the Rebels [Montrose's army]', continuing that he attempted to persuade the

---

[41] When considering this point it should also be considered that in the confusion of battle it would have been very difficult for any army commander to exercise full control over all the forces under his command in the seventeenth century

[42] It should be remembered that the Covenanter government in Scotland had dispatched an army to England under the act of Solemn League and Covenant of September 1643

Earl of Calendar to 'undertake charge of that war [the impending continuation of the campaign against Montrose]' (Napier, c1838). The source Napier (c1838) asserts that Baillie goes on to state that he was 'pressed', even 'forced', to undertake command of the army and goes on to assert that the occasion for Argyle to command behind the scenes whilst Baillie served as figurehead commander, under Argyle's orders, did not materialise into actuality as Baillie would not consent to receiving orders from Argyle (Napier, c1838).

To further address the question of who was in command of the Covenanter army it is necessary to briefly look at the Covenanter political system. The Triennial Act that had been formulated as a centerpiece of Covenanter government stipulated that parliament had to meet at least once every three years in order 'to preserve religion, administer justice, remedy grievances and suppress corruption' (APS, v, 268 & Volume 18, GSC 1637-1651, XXV, 1982). The initial function of the Committee of Estates was to provide effective rule for Scotland at times when parliament had dissolved (Volume 18, GSC 1637-1651, XXV, 1982). In reality, the Committee of Estates was a form of dictatorship, even having a military flavour to it. This was born of the fact that a committee consisting of twelve nobbles, three lords of session, thirteen barons and twelve burgesses would be added to by the inclusion of general officers of the army.[43] This committee had the power to 'direct and govern the whole country [the kingdom of Scotland]' (Volume 18, GSC 1637-1651, XXVI, 1982). The committee itself, although sold as a singular entity, was in fact split in two, one section remaining with parliament and the other accompanying the army (APS, v, 282-4). The committee was widely regarded by its detractors as being nothing more than a replacement for direct Royal rule that enabled a handful of upper echelon covenanters to rule the country with the Committee of Estates being merely a front. Such a mechanism was, in theory, meant to have been put in place as a temporary measure, until such time as a settlement could be reached between Parliament and the King, Charles I (Volume 18, GSC 1637-1651, XXVI, 1982).

The Royalist threat to Covenanter rule in Scotland had grown in scale during the winter of 1644-45. Montrose's victories over the covenanters had effectively destroyed the latter's power base throughout much of the North of Scotland (Volume 18, GSC 1637-1651, 1, 1982). A new commission of the Committee of the Estates was granted by the 28th Act of the first session of the first triennial parliament on 8 March 1645. This commission called for the Committee of Estates to:

> "... do all and everything requisite concerning the ordering and managing of all affairs and business which might conduce to the good and peace of the kingdom [Scotland] and promoting the common cause as expressed in the [Solemn League and] covenant and treaties" (P.A.12/I, min 16-31 Oct 1645; P.A.11/4, fos. 13IV-176V & Volume 18, GSC 1637-1651, 3, 1982).

The main Committee of the Estates was combined with the Covenanter army in Scotland under a single committee by a decision of parliament issued on 7 August

---

[43] When conceived, nobbles, barons and burgesses made up the three estates of the Committee of Estates (Volume 18, GSC 1637-1651, XXIV, 1982)

1645 (Volume 18, GSC 1637-1651, 1, 1982). This committee would accompany the army in the field, the commander in chief of that army having recourse to consult with the committee on matters pertaining to the army's employment. This was designed to produce a single authority responsible for confronting the army of Montrose. This has been justified, at least in part, by the fact that the relocation of Parliament from the Edinburgh [due to pestilence] had effectively dismantled the mechanism of the two committee system of a fixed location central committee and a mobile committee accompanying the army (Volume 18, GSC 1637-1651, 1, 1982). The danger of the single committee system was that should disaster befall the army then it would effectively befall the civil government (Volume 18, GSC 1637-1651, 1, 1982) and the civil and army committee's being amalgamated into one lay open the route to accusations of military dictatorship. The 7 August 1645 decision effectively stated that 'parliament or its committees were responsible for directing the war against Montrose, but the commanding general was responsible for the actual managing and execution (APS, VI, I, 448) of such directions' (Volume 18, GSC 1637-1651, xlv, 1982). This decision showed that parliament had a distinct lack of confidence in the Covenanter generals, a situation no doubt brought about by successive defeats against Montrose. The 7 August decision produced a situation of confusion in regard to civil authority and military authority, this, no doubt, contributing to the decisive defeat suffered by the Covenanters at Kilsyth just over one week later (Volume 18, GSC 1637-1651, XIV).

The evidence then shows that prior to his defeat to Montrose at the battle of Alford Baillie was in command of the Covenanter army, but with recourse to respect the wants of the Committee of Estates as decreed by Parliament (Napier, c1839 & Baillie, 1841-1842). Following his petition to be exonerated of blame for his defeat at Alford, Ballie was sent back to the Covenanter army, but he had to accede to the wants of the main Committee of the Estates rather than just take their advice and recommendations (Volume 18, GSC 1637-1651, 1982, Napier, c1838 & Baillie, 1841-1842). Similar situations still arise in the modern world whereby military commanders do not have the authority to act as they see fit, but rather have to accede to the instructions of their political masters, whom, in this case, accompanied the army in the field. In this respect, however, Baillie was still in command of the army, not Argyle, as is often stated, for the 7 August act defined clearly Baillie's authority once the decision had been taken by the committee to commit the army to battle as he, as the commanding General, would bear responsibility for the actual managing and execution of the military operation (APS, VI, I, 448). Therefore, once Baillie acceded to the wants of the Committee of Estates – to take battle to Montrose at Kilsyth – the responsibility for the disposition of the Covenanter army lay entirely with him as the commanding General. That Baillie was retained in this de-facto command role following previous defeats speaks volumes for the fact that the pool of capable Generals was so poor on the Covenanter side that they could not afford to lose him.

BAILLIE MARCHES ON KILSYTH FROM THE NORTH EAST

Ballie was reliant on reinforcements from Fife to ensure a sizeable margin of superiority in numbers for his army over that of Montrose's army. To this end, the Earl of Crawford was dispatched to Coupar to ascertain when the Fife Regiments would effect junction with Baillie's army – this junction was affected the following day at Rossie, Fife, although, in the pursuit of Montrose's army, the Fife regiments would trail in the rear of Baillie's main force[44] (Baillie, 1841-1842). As it approached Stirling the Covenanter army camped between the settlement of Sauchie and the bridge at Tullibody.[45] The following day Baillie was informed that Montrose's army had crossed the River Forth to the North of Stirling and the Committee of Estates advised that Baillie should also cross the Forth at Stirling. Baillie halted his army of five Regiments 'a little above the parke, upon the South West side' of Stirling whilst he awaited the arrival of the three Regiments raised in Fife, which were following in his rear (Baillie, 1841-1842). It was at this point that Baillie was informed that Montrose was marching across the hills toward Kilsyth.

On hearing that Montrose was marching on Kilsyth Baillie, following consultation with the Committee of Estates, ordered his army to march on Denny, around 8 km or so to the North East of Kilsyth, and crossed the River Carron at the Bridge located there. The Covenanter army them moved to a location referred to as Hollin-Buss (Holland Bush), around 3 km (2 miles) eastward of Kilsyth, where the it camped on the night of 14 August as the Royalist army waited at Kilsyth (Baillie, 1841-1842).[46]

OPPOSING FORCES

The exact composition of the forces of the opposing sides that were present at Kilsyth is vague to say the least. While we can more or less give numbers in regiments, such a word in an enigma in regards to numbers of men under each command. Rarely would two regiments be the same in number in an army such as that of Montrose as regiments were nominally formed from the areas of the various Earls and Marquis, while others would be recruited along the way as a particular army marched, this latter recruitment tactic being employed to replenished or swell the ranks of the army. An upper end value put the army of Montrose at 5,000 foot and 500 horse and that of Baillie at 6,000 foot and 500 horse (The History of the Scottish Wars, 1825). Another account puts the Royalist army at 4,400 foot and 500 horse troops and that of the Covenanters at 6,000 foot and 800 horse troops. This is close to the upper end value of 7,000 all arms for the Covenanter army put forward

[44] Rossie lies on a line about 15 km South eastward of Perth and about 8 km South westward of Cupar. Cupar lies on a line about 20 km South eastward of Perth

[45] Sauchie lies under 1 km northward of Alloa and about 2 km or so from Tullibody. Tullibody lies just over 3 km to eastward and a little northward of Stirling and about 2 km North westward of Alloa

[46] Hollin-Buss (Holland Bush) lies about 3 km eastward of Kilsyth. The site of the Covenanter encampment is thought to be several hundred metres North of the modern day town of Banknock, which lies a similar distance eastward of Kilsyth to the 1645 Hollin Buss

by a Bishop Guthrie. The large size of the Covenanter army was due to the joining together of several commands. The value of 4,400 and 500 foot and horse troops respectively is considered accurate by what is stated as an old historian of the Gordon family (Napier, c1838), but caution should be exercised as no name has been forwarded for this source.

While we can be reasonably confident in the value of 6,500-7,000 all arms for the Covenanter army, it is somewhat more complicated in attempting to arrive at a realistic value for the numbers in the army of Montrose. The estimate for the number of troops (horse and foot) available to Montrose at Auldearn was 2,000-3,000 (Napier, c1838). Although Royalist casualties at Auldearn were described as low we have to take into account the depletion of the ranks due to Aboyne and the bulk of the highland troops in Montrose's army returning home after crossing the Grampians (Napier, c1838). This would have vastly reduced Montrose's available force by around one third and perhaps as much as half. If we take the value of 2,000-3,000 troops available at Auldearn then this could have now been reduced to 1,500-2,000, or perhaps less. Aboyne rejoined Montrose, as did some of the Gordon horse troops, as the Royalist army marched to confront Baillie at Alford (Napier, c1838), but the source for this does not provide numbers. For the battle of Alford it would be difficult to accept that Montrose had available more than 3,000 foot and horse troops, a value of 2,300-2,400 all-arms being more likely. We do not have reliable figures for Royalist fatalities, or those *Hors de Combat*, at Alford, but it is accepted that they were light. However, if we consider that Montrose had a low value of 250 horse[47] at Alford then the casualties may have been higher than reported if we accept the statement that following the battle of Alford Montrose had only about 100 horse troop's available (The History of the Scottish Wars, 1825). If, following the battle of Alford, we consider that Montrose had perhaps 2,200 troops (horse and foot) available, we can build up a picture of his likely force as he retired to Kilsyth. We are informed that Montrose received reinforcements from Athol when he was in the area of Angus, but numbers are not provided. We are informed that Macdonald also rejoined Montrose at Angus, bringing with him 700 Maclean's, 500 Clanranald's, 500 from Glengarry and smaller numbers from the McGregor's, Macnabs some Macphersons and Farquharsons (Napier, c1838). We can assume that this increased Montrose's available force by perhaps 2,000-2200, which, added to his estimated force of perhaps 2,200, would provide a force of 4,400. This would be in the ballpark of the estimate of 4,000-5,000 provided by in the account of the source (Napier, c1838). Considering that many of the highland/northern[48] troops had left the army a

---

[47] Some accounts credit Montrose's army with about 500 horse troops at Alford. However, in the absence of supporting evidence, such a high value has to be considered very unlikely

[48] Some accounts refer to highland troops while others refer to northern troops. It is assumed that these are meant to be one in the same – highland troops. However, the north of Scotland and the highland fault line are different geographically. As an example the southern western Isles are part of the Highlands (termed Highlands and Islands) whilst part of Aberdeenshire, which lies several hundred kilometres farther North is part of the Lowlands

value closer to the 4,000-4,500 is probably the most accurate. However, to this value can be added a further body of 100 horse troops from the Gordons's. While some historians put the overall number of troops available to Montrose at this time at around 6,000, such a value would be reached only by adding the numbers that Montrose possessed at Auldearn (2,000-3,000) to the numbers of Highlanders that joined the standard at Angus, the 100 or so provided by the Gordons and perhaps 1200 foot and 300 horse later provided by Aboyne and the Earl of Airlie, but not available to Montrose as he threatened Perth. It fails to take into consideration the natural wastage through those leaving the ranks after Auldearn. As previously noted, we have to accept that in the absence of complete records the true number of troops, particularly with the army of Montrose, at the various battles of the campaign, particularly Alford and Kilsyth, will never be known with any high degree of confidence. The 4,000-4,600 troops available to Montrose were increased by around 200 cavalry and 100 mounted Musketeers and a further 80 or so Cavalry from the Ogilvie's, which arrived with the Earl of Airlie (The History of the Scottish Wars, 1825 & Napier, c1838). This would have increased Montrose's total available force to around 5,000.[49]

ROYALIST REGIMENTS

It is unknown what regimental system the Royalist troops were arrayed in at Kilsyth. Montrose was the commander in chief of the Royalist army. Alasdair MacColla still commanded the Scottish and Irish Gaels, but subordinate to Montrose. We know the Irish Gael's remained with the army, but to say they remained in a three regiment formation as had previously been the case would be pure conjecture. There were also several regiments of Highlanders available and some Lowlanders making up the rest of the army. One regiment at Kilsyth was commanded by Lieutenant Colonel William Farquharson of Inverey[50] (SHS Vol. 41 & Mosley, 2003). Other commanders at Kilsyth included the Earl of Airlie, Macdonald, Aboyne and clan chiefs mentioned when Montrose received his reinforcements North of the Forth.

COVENANTER REGIMENTS

The significant commanders on the Covenanter side were Baillie (commander in chief), the Marquis of Argyle (regimental), Earl of Tullibardine (regimental), Lord Balcarres (regimental), Lord Burleigh (regimental), Lord Elcho (regimental) the Earl of Crawford (Lindsay) (Napier, c1838 & Baillie, 1841-1842). Of these only Lindsay had not been present at an outright Covenanter defeat at the hands of Montrose's

---

[49] As recorded throughout the text some historians accept a larger value for the number of men available to Montrose

[50] Also reported as having participated in the battles at Aberdeen, Auldearn and Alford (Scottish History Society Vol.41)

army. Despite the previous victories for Montrose, the creed for the Covenanter army appeared to be to carry the day through overwhelming force of arms – the many being stronger than the fewer. It was the knowledge that Montrose's army was numerically weaker than the Covenanter army that may have driven Argyle, supported by the other members of the Committee of Estates, to be so confident in taking the battle to the Royalist army at Kilsyth, despite the unsuitability of the lay of the land for an attacking force.

While our knowledge of the regimental system for the Royalist army is ambiguous we can, with confidence, detail the number of Covenanter regiments at Kilsyth on 15 August 1645. We are told that the Covenanter army had been significantly reinforced by three regiments raised in Fife (Napier, c1838 & Baillie, 1841-1842) and a further regiment consisting of Highlanders (Campbell's) of the Marquis of Argyle (Napier, c1838). While the three Fife regiments would form Baillie's reserve at Kilsyth, the Marquis of Argyle's regiment of Highlanders would form a part of the main line in company with four other regiments. This five forward and three reserve regiment constitution of the Covenanter army at Kilsyth is confirmed by documentary evidence in the form of Ballie's letters. Modern age assertions that ten Covenanter regiments were present is not supported by documentary evidence. In the absence of supporting evidence we must accept the contemporary evidence that shows the five forward regiments and three reserve regiments for a total of eight regiments in the Covenanter order of battle at Kilsyth. The commanders of the forward regiments, as confirmed by Ballie's letter documents, were the Marquis of Argyle (Archibald Campbell), the Earl of Lauderdale (John Maitland), Lord Balcarres, Colonell (Colonel) Robert Hume (Home)[51] and the Earl of Crawford (Ludovick Lindsay) (Baillie, 1841-1842). The issue of command of the fifth regiment has been a point of historical debate with names such as a Colonell Kennedy being forward in some writings. However, the evidence from Baillie himself confirms, unequivocally, that the Earl of Crawford was in command of the fifth regiment. There were certainly other regimental commanders (more accurately former regimental commanders) present including a Colonel Robert Cunningham with the remnants of his regiment, which had been seriously weakened at the battle of Alford and incorporated within other regiments.[52] The three Fife regiments that formed Baillie's reserve were under the overall command of a General-Major Leslie, this confirmed in Baillie's letter documents – page 422 (Baillie, 1841-1842). While Baillie's accounts do not confirm same, Elcho and Burleigh were probably in command of individual reserve regiments as they often accompanied Baillie in the field at Kilsyth, an indicator of reserve status awaiting instructions. The Earl of Crawford's regiment was heavy in cavalry that could be used to exploit an enemy weakness or plug a gap in the covenanter line,

---

[51] It is suggested that some 200 men of the Earl of Glencairn's regiment were transferred from service in Ireland to Hume (Home's) regiment in time for the battle at Kilsyth

[52] We know that the remnants of Cunningham's regiment that had survived the battle of Alford were present at Kilsyth (Volume 18, GSC 1637-1651, 1982) along with contingents of other Covenanter regiments decimated in previous battles against Montrose's army

backed up by the three reserve regiments.

THE MYTH OF THE NAKED ARMY

Before moving onto the battle at Kilsyth itself the matter of the naked army myth that has surrounded the Royalist army at Kilsyth will be addressed. The evidence strongly suggest the myth of the naked army is just that, a myth. It has to be considered that both of Baillie's reports on the battle fail to address this point. The most plausible reason for this is that there was nothing to address. Had the Covenanter army been charged by several thousand naked men, this would surely have warranted a mention in Baillie's reports. It is, however, perfectly plausible, even probable, that Montrose instructed his foot troops in particular to discard heavy garments to aid ease of movement and mobility in the heat of an August day. This would increase not only the fighting efficiency, but the endurance of the men who would be expected to pursue a fleeing enemy if Baillie's army was to be destroyed and not just driven from the field.[53] Such practices are common in the modern age when soldiers discard unnecessary equipment and garments before attacking an enemy position on foot. While the counter-insurgency conflicts of western armies in recent decades have little requirement for this practice, during the Cold War years it was common practice to discard heavy clothing during very hot weather operations in the British army.[54] On examination of the naked army myth it has to be said, quite emphatically, that the evidence does not support the claim that the Royalist army, due to the extreme heat of the day, stripped off most of their cloths prior to the battle proper.

THE LOCATION OF THE COMMENCEMENT OF THE BATTLE

The area where the battle is thought have taken place is around 250 m to the east of modern day Kilsyth. This would have been perhaps 600 m ± 100 m from the Kilsyth of 1645. The distance from the ground battle is thought to have been fought on to Dullatur bog would have been 500-900 m ± 100 m. The uncertainty is due to the fact that the exact location of the battle is a major point of contention in hysterography. That there is disagreement as to the specific location of the battlefield is not unusual for an area so radically changed from the way it was more than three and a half centuries before.

Employing investigation of modern day topography, what is known of the

---

[53] The Royalist cause required not just a victory at Kilsyth, but the destruction of the Covenanter army so it did not face any significant threat in its rear as it advanced on England to confront the Scottish Covenanter army supporting the English Parliamentarians fighting the Royalists of Charles I under the act of Solemn League and Covenant of September 1643

[54] The author's observation is made from personal experience of serving as an infantry soldier in the Argyle and Sutherland Highlanders. The thick cotton shirts of the British army uniform would often be removed leaving only the outer combat jacket during operations in very warm weather

topography of 1645 and the reports of the time, provide a better understanding of where the battle took place. We know the Covenanter army advance toward Kilsyth was conducted through corn fields, but we do not have definitive information as to where the corn fields themselves ended. We can rule out the glen as an area of corn field growing as this would not have been a location for growing corn.[55] The suggested dispositions of the two armies shown in an overview map from Historic Scotland in reference to Reid (2003) has to be considered improbable as this put the two armies far too close together – barely 100 m separating them – at start lines. Baillie's own reports on the battle refer to Concenter musketeers firing without orders when well out of effective musket range, which would completely rule out such close dispositions.[56] Another indicator that the secondary dispositions shown in Reid (2003) are improbably is that the lines of attack would effectively show the Royalist initial start line 100 m forward of Slaughter Howe, about 250+ m to the North.

The dispositions in the Historic Scotland map suggested by Seymour (1979) may be nearer the mark in that they were further southward, but this would put the main body of the Royalist army inside and across the width of the glen that was located on the site where the reservoir is today. This is unlikely as it would have produced enormous disadvantages to the Royalist foot in having to scramble up the glen walls in an attack on the Covenanter main body not to mention the fact that the view of an attacking Covenanter army would have been obscured by the glen walls for much of the Royalist main body. It would also have invited destruction of the Royalist army in the event of a successful Covenanter flanking attack, there being little to no chance for the army to retire. We can further rule out the Royalist army being deployed almost wholesale within the Glen through information furnished in Baillie's reports, which refer only to small bands of Royalist foot troops advancing up the glen in irregular fashion. Seymour (1979) is probably the most sound in regard to lines of advance in attack by the Royalist troops. This shows not only the Royalist cavalry attack that supported the foot to the left of the Royalist main line, resulting in rout of the Covenanter army, but also the Royalist infiltration up the glen (the modern day reservoir) to the southward, clearly detailed in Baillie's reports of the battle.

The most likely disposition was the Covenanter army at the eastern end of the modern day reservoir, but perhaps extending 50-100 m or so further northward. The

---

[55] We have no information regarding the status of the corn – had it been harvested or was it still in pre-harvest growth – August being a month that it could have been harvested. If it had not been harvested we are also not privy to the height of the corn which can grow taller than a man. This information itself is purely academic if the corn fields that the Covenanter army advanced through were to the east of the battlefield locality

[56] There are a number of modern day estimates and reports from contemporary to early Twentieth century sources for effective range of a mid-Seventeenth century musket. These range from a few hundred metres out to around 400 metres. The discrepancy may be due to inaccurate information or, perhaps, differences in what is meant by effective range

Royalist army was initially well out of musket range, probably near the western end of the modern day reservoir, and, as with the Covenanter army, 50-100 m or so to the northward of the modern day reservoir. In this respect, the area referred to as Slaughter Howe is considerably North of the main dispositions. We cannot place any reliance on names attached to certain locations considerable periods of time after the battle - 'Slaughter Howe', Baggage Knowe' and 'Bullet Knowe' for example. If we assign credibility to these then we must move the battle up to 500 m further West to cover a place referred to as 'Cavalry Park'. Until recent decades this was a pasture for cattle before being developed for residential housing in the Twenty first century. Named after the cavalry charge of the Royalist army, this site has no credibility as the site of said cavalry charge which we know through the accounts attributed to Montrose and the reports of Baillie, took place to the North of the glen – the modern day reservoir. If Cavalry Park was accepted as the location of the Royalist charge we would also have to move the battle ~500 m to the South to allow Cavalry Park to remain to the North of the two armies – this would place the battle in the middle of the blogland, which we know could not have been the location, further discrediting Cavalry Park's credibility as a location of any significance to the battle. Furthermore, the area referred to as 'Bullet Knowe', located about 300 m South of the modern day reservoir (the 1645 glen would also be too far South). There is no reference to any major action taking place that far south of the glen in any contemporary accounts of the battle. As is the case with the other areas named after the battle, Bullet Knowes was allocated some considerable after the events of 1645.[57]

We also have the oft referred to hill that was the centre of the initial struggle between the opposing armies. While Slaughter Howe could be called a rise, it is a stretch, in 2018, to call it a hill, and, as it is undeveloped and not cultivated farmland, it must remain today much as it was in 1645. A 373 year period is a mere second on a geological timescale – not enough time has elapsed for geological process to have significantly reduced or increased its elevation. Another potential candidate for the contested hill is located on the North East shore of the modern day reservoir – the 1645 glen. More than three centuries of cultivation would be expected to reduce the prominence of the hill, but certainly not remove it. On the surface this may seem like a good indicator that the hill on the North shore near the eastern end of the modern day reservoir may be the hill in question that was on the eastern end of the North side of the 1645 glen. We must, of course, err on the side of caution as it is possible that human developments associated with the build of the reservoir have affected the elevation of this location upward or downward. Indeed, the work connected with the construction of the reservoir in the late Eighteenth century may well be entirely responsible for the formation of this hill. Without an archaeological dig at this site it is not possible to determine whether this hill was formed through natural processes prior to 1645 or formed solely or in part by human activity in the Eighteenth century. However, in the absence of archaeological evidence, we cannot ignore the hill as a candidate as the hill that was recorded as having been contested in Baillie's reports. That said, the hill is much closer to the glen (the modern day reservoir) than

---

[57] The word bullet was not in use in regard to firearm ammunition until the mid-nineteenth century

would be inferred from Ballie's reports. At the opposite end of the scale the area known as 'Slaughter Howe' would appear to be too far North of the glen, as noted above. While 'Slaughter Howe' as the site of the contested hill, is supported by modern local authority maps showing the position of Montrose's standard as 400-500 m North of the glen and around 100 m westward, there is no documentary evidence to support this as being the position of Montrose's standard. It seems likely that this position has been selected for the maps due to it being west of 'Slaughter Howe', as previously noted, portrayed as the scene of the contested hill described in Baillie's reports of the battle.

A geophysical investigations may identify the positions and lines of advance of the dykes in those areas of the battlefield not submerged or subjected to intensive human development. This may aid in better identifying the initial defensive positions – start points – of the Royalist army and, therefore, the lines of attack of the Covenanter army and the counter attack of the Royalist army. This would then help in confirming or refuting 'Slaughter Howe's' credibility as the location the hill contested at the start of the battle. Modern field boundaries are of no use to the historian as an indicator of the exact locations of the 1645 boundaries imposed by the stone dykes referred to in reports of the battle. A geophysical investigation or an old fashioned archeological dig would provide a better picture of 1645 field boundary and enclosure dykes. Until such an investigation is conducted the exact locations of the various stages of battle will come down to guesswork based on an examination of modern topography and what we can understand about the 1645 topography combined with the battle reports of that day.

It is the location of the glen – the modern day reservoir that provides us with the best indicators of where the various attacks took place. This also provides a better understanding of the best candidates for the start positions for both armies, but with the aforementioned degree of uncertainty.

BAILLIE AT KILSYTH

Around dawn on the morning of 15 August 1645[58], the Marquis of Argyle, in company with Lord Burleigh (Baillie, in his account, states that he could not remember if it was Burleigh or some other person), went to Baillie's tent and asked the location of the rebels (Montrose's army). After Baillie informed him that they were still at Kilsyth, Argyle asked 'if we [the Covenanter army] might not advance nearer them' to which Baillie replied 'we are near enough if we intended not to fight, and that his Lordship knew well enough how rough and uneasie [uneasy] a way that was to march in'. Argyle replied 'we need not keep the hie-way [road], bot [but] march over at nearest' (Baillie, 1841-1842). This last statement indicates the intention not to advance along the carriage track from Hollin Buss to Kilsyth, but to advance across the land slightly to the North of the track (a combination of rough natural

---

[58] On 15 August 2018, sunrise in the general area of Kilsyth is put at 05.48 hours, but for 15 August 1645 this would have been 04.46 am ± 2 minutes

ground and corn fields) that would bring the Covenanter army through the area that is the modern day Banton village around 2 km to the west of Hollin Buss and around 2 km to the East of Montrose's army waiting at Kilsyth. Baillie asked for the Earle of Crawford and several others to be called from the next tent, those gentlemen expressing their desire, in line with Argyle, to advance on the Royalist army at Kilsyth Baillie, 1841-1842).

On the realisation that the Covenanter army was preparing to give battle on the morning of 15 August, Montrose is stated to have declared 'So much the better... it is the very thing I want, and as for their numbers [a reference to the fact that the Covenanter army was superior in numbers compared to the Royalist army], we have the best ground, which is more than half the battle' (Napier, c1838). Montrose set about his own preparations to meet the covenanter army. He ordered that advantageous ground between the two armies be occupied by groups of Royalist troops.[59] The field was rural in nature save a few scattered houses, which were occupied by Royalist forces (Napier, c1838).

Although we are not privy to timings, we are informed that Baillie, at the behest of the Committee of Estates, commenced his advance westward through corn fields toward Kilsyth. During this advance several nobbles of the Committee (Baillie states he could not remember their names, therefore we have to eliminate Argyle as it seems inconceivable that Baillie would forget his presence) came to Baillie and asked for permission to send forces up a small hill located on the right hand side of the Covenanter army line of advance. Baillie replied that he 'did not conceive that ground to be good, and that the rebells [rebels] (if they would) might possess themselves of it before us [the covenanter army]' (Baillie, 1841-1842). However, on the suggestion of one of the nobbles (Baillie again provides no name) a small force was sent to reconnoiter the hill in question. Around this time Baillie moved, along with Lord Elcho and Lord Burleigh, to the 'right hand of the [Covenanter] regiments' (Baillie, 1841-1842). A short time after arriving on the right, Baillie, still in company with Lords Elcho and Burleigh, was requested to join other noble's, assumedly, further to the left of the direction of march. The nobles that had called for Baillie were of the opinion that some advantage could be made against the Royalist army if pressed. This was not to Baillie's liking and he informed them that he considered the enemy would have the advantage and that even if the Covenanters arrived at the aforementioned hill in advance of Royalist forces, this hill would be of little advantage to the Covenanters. A recourse to accede to the demands of a majority of what members of the Committee of Estates was at hand (this included Argyle, the Earls of Crawford and Tullibardine and Lords Elcho and Burleigh, along with unnamed others) led Baillie to accept their desire to advance on the hill (only Balcarres is known to have sided with Baillie in being against this course of action).[60]

---

[59] There is no documentary evidence in regard to the strength of these groups

[60] This appears to contradict the decision of Parliament of 7 August 1645 that ruled 'parliament or its committees were responsible for directing the war against Montrose, but the commanding general was responsible for the actual managing and execution' (APS, VI, I, 448) of such directions

Ballie gives the following description of this advance:

"The commanded men, with the horsemen, marched before; the regiment on the right hand, faceing [facing] to the right hand, and so the rest advanced to the hill; where, I suppose, that was done by me which was incumbent unto me in all that the shortness of time would suffer before we were engaged" (Baillie, 1841-1842)

There were in actuality two official accounts of the battle forwarded by Baillie – the first proving to be inadequate to satisfy parliament, resulting in a second paper being drawn up to elaborate further on the movements of the army on that fateful day. In this second paper Baillie elaborated on sending, at the behest of the Committee, a party of musketeers to the hill on the right of the Covenanter line of advance. He further elaborated that a Major Halden was allocated to guide the musketeers toward an enclosure and confirms that this was carried out. He then goes on to state that he 'followed them immediately with my Lord Balcarres and the horsemen, giving order for the foot to follow' (Baillie, 1841-1842). Baillie then recounts his arrival at a group of 'gentlemen on horseback' and noted that musketeers were firing shot at random, presumably, although this is not confirmed, in the direction of the out of effective range Royalist troops. Baillie goes to great length to point out that this was done without any order being issued by him. He then recounts how he, in company with Lord Burleigh and the Earl of Crawford, proceeded on horseback 'over the brae [slope]' in order to observe the position of the Royalist troops 'embattled in the meadow' and noted that 'sundries of them disbanded, were falling up the glen through the bushes' (Baillie, 1841-1842). The choice of wording here suggests, strongly, that these small groups of Royalists were moving in a disorganised manner, although in what direction is not made clear, the most plausible being toward the Covenanter line. Baillie and his party then returned to the 'braehead' (brow of hill) where they found the Marquis of Argyle and several other unnamed gentlemen. A Major Halden was observed taking a body of musketeers of undetermined strength across a field in the direction of an isolated house close to the glen, it being pointed out by Baillie that this was done without orders from him. Baillie goes on to state of Major Halden and his body of musketeers that they failed to retire even after he had dispatched, first, Colonell Arnot and then Rootmaster Blair, to bring them back. Baillie then notes that he wanted Halden's party to retire as a strong body of Royalist's (this would be foot troops) had taken up position to oppose them. Baillie, in company with Balcarres, returned to the Covenanter regiments, whereby, on having requested instructions, he ordered Balcarres to 'draw up his regiment on the right hand of the Earl of Lauderdale's [regiment]' (Baillie, 1841-1842). Baillie then provided orders to Lauderdale, in person and through his adjutant, as follows: '... face to the right hand, and to march to the foot of the hill, then to face as they were [this order is ambiguous, but is taken to mean to face westward again]'; orders for Hume were 'to follow their [Lauderdale's regiment] steps, halt when they halted, and keep distance and front with them' (Baillie, 1841-1842). Baillie then states that 'The Marquis [and] his Major, as I went toward him, asked what he should do?' (Baillie, 1841-1842). Baillie instructed him to take position on the left of Hume's regiment and then departed. Baillie then states that he was not at a great distance from the Marquis of Argyle when he looked back and observed that 'Hume had left the way' that Baillie had instructed for him to take and was galloping 'right west' which took him to an area of dykes and toward the Royalist army[61] (Baillie, 1841-1842). Baillie goes on to state that he turned to follow after Hume and, on meeting the Adjutant, gave orders for him to arrange for the Earl of Crawford's regiment to take position on the left of Lauderdale's regiment and that the three Fyfe regiments should continue to hold position in reserve under General-Major Leslie (Baillie, 1841-1842). The Early of Crawford's regiment was required to take this position to fill any gap that was forming between Hume and Lauderdale's regiments through Hume's unordered march toward the Royalist line. Before Hume could be recalled Baillie states:

"he [Hume] and the other two regiments, to wit [which], the Marquess [Marquis] of Argyle's, and the three that were joined in one, had taken in ane [an] inclosure [enclosure], from whilk [which] (the enemy being so near) it was impossible to bring them off' (Baillie, 1841-1842).

In a short time the Royalist foot had approached to another dyke nearer the Covenanter regiments, musketeers of which were firing in the direction of the Royalist line to such an extent that Baillie exhorted in his report that they 'made more fire than I could have wished', but this was to no effect as they were too far from their intended targets[62] (Baillie, 1841-1842). Baillie states that he, 'with the assistance of such officers as were known unto me' attempted, with little success, to stem the firing to save shot until such time as the Royalist army was within effective range Baillie, 1841-1842). The stage was set for the rout of the Covenanter regiments. Before much time had passed the Royalist foot scrambled over the dyke and charged headlong against the Covenanter regiments, which quickly broke. Baillie proceeded on horseback to the aforementioned brae where he came across General-Major Hollburne (this gentleman was on his own), whom brought Baillie's attention to a 'squadron of rebells horsemen, who had gone by and charged the horsemen with Lieutenant-Colonell Murray' (Baillie, 1841-1842). It is these Royalist horsemen that Baillie considers continued on to rout the Earl of Crawford's cavalry.

BAILLIE'S RETIREMENT FROM THE FIELD

In his first account Baillie states that he retired from the battlefield 'on the rear of the horses of the rebells [rebels] who broke the Earl of Crawford [cavalry]' after

---

[61] This statement would confirm that the Royalist army was positioned West of the Covenanter army and therefore rules out the Covenanter to the North and Royalist to the South dispositions put forward by some historians. Hume not following Lauderdale's steps in facing right (turning North) and marching toward the hill before turning to face West again would have left a gap between the two regiments

[62] Considering that after an advance from the Royalist start line that they were still out of musket range it would rule out a certain dispositions mentioned above, which put the two armies initial start lines as barely 100 m apart

three Regiments, including Hume's and Argyle's had been broken and taken to flight (Baillie, 1841-1842).[63] In his second account Baillie, as noted above, states that his attention was brought to a body of Royalist cavalry that went on to rout the Earl of Crawford's cavalry, Baillie retiring, in company with a Major-General Hollburne, to the rear to join with the three reserve regiments only to find that these regiments had taken flight. Attempts to arrest the flight and get even a small party of the reserve to stand to cover the line of retreat (this is more accurately referred to as flight) proved impossible as panic had overtaken the Covenanter troops, and every man with a horse was making hast away from the battlefield. All being lost, Baillie, still in company with Hollburne, and now joined with some officers of the reserve regiments, took flight, reaching the Bridge across the River Kelvin at Denny where Baillie and Hollburne parted from the aforementioned officers of the reserve regiments and rode on to Stirling (Baillie, 1841-1842).

INFORMATION FROM THE ROYALIST ACCOUNT OF THE BATTLE

The fighting would commence with Covenanter attempts to overrun the few Royalist strongholds between the two armies (Napier, c1838). The Royalist defence of these strongholds would prove pivotal to the outcome of the battle, for, on seeing the Covenanters forced back from the strongholds a body of highlanders, estimated at around 1,000 in number, from the Royalist ranks, scrambled across the dykes and charged headlong uphill toward the Covenanter regiments facing them. This lack of discipline in the ranks of the highlanders apparently caused Montrose no little anxiety, particularly when a considerable force of Covenanter foot, supported by several troops of Covenanter cavalry (this was from the Early of Crawford's regiment) began moving forward to meet the highlanders uncoordinated attack (Napier, c1838). At this point Montrose ordered the Earl of Airlie to support the highlanders attack with his cavalry, apparently saying to the elderly Earl[64], 'the eyes and wishes of the whole army are upon you my Lord Airly [Airlie], as the person most capable by your authority, discretion, and bravery, to save these men, and redeem the day from their want of discipline' (Napier, c1838). Airlie took the task and ordered a troop of cavalry, commanded by John Ogilvy of Baldavie, to advance. This troop promptly charged the Covenanter cavalry that was supporting the Covenanter foot troops advance against the highlanders.[65] The source SHS Volume 51-53 (1906) states that Airlie came to the aid of Montrose's troops that were under attack and close to being surrounded and overrun by an estimated 2,000-3,000 covenanters, including cavalry (that of the Earl of Crawford) (SHS Volume 51-53,

[63] A General-Major Hollburne is mentioned at this juncture in such a manner that it could be inferred that he was a regimental commander. However, as noted in the main text Baillie clearly states the commanders of the five main regiments. In this respect it may be assumed that Hollburne was a subordinate commander or in command of the third reserve regiment

[64] Airlie was around 70 years old. (Volume 51-53, 282 (340)

[65] John Ogilvy had formerly served in the Swedish army with the rank of Colonel

1906). While the upper end estimate of the strength of Covenanter troops involved in this part of the battle may be contested, what is not in doubt is that this action set the scene for rout of the Covenanter army at Kilsyth. The Royalist cavalry broke the Covenanter cavalry, which turned and rode into the oncoming Covenanter foot troops, throwing then into confusion and outright panic. From this point the day was with the Royalist army as more of the Royalist foot charged the wavering ranks of the Covenanter regiments, which were broken as confusion and panic turned to flight (Napier, c1838). The Covenanter foot troops were abandoned by most of the nobbles whom elected to save themselves, most making for the sanctuary of the castle at Stirling. The source Napier (c1838) states that Argyle, in company with several other nobbles, made for the Forth and boarded a vessel that was lain at anchor in the estuary. The master of this ship was ordered to way anchor and put to sea, but the above mentioned source fails to provide a destination or, indeed the name of the ship, therefore caution should be observed when considering its accuracy (Napier, c1838).

Even getting around the old Scots language Baillie's letter reports are as confusing as they are bereft of legible tactical description in many areas. However, it has to be accepted that Baillie could not be everywhere at once and we are not privy to what information that he was furnished with by his subordinates. Particularly once the rout commenced, the scene would have been chaotic to say the least. Baillie also expends enormous energy of purpose in his letter reports in attempting to cover himself, indeed, absolve himself of responsibility for the disaster that befell the Covenanter army on that fateful day. An important point that should be made is that at times neither of the commanders of the opposing armies were able to exert operational control over much of their forces from the commencement of battle.[66]

---

[66] Both commanders admit as much in their reports of the battle

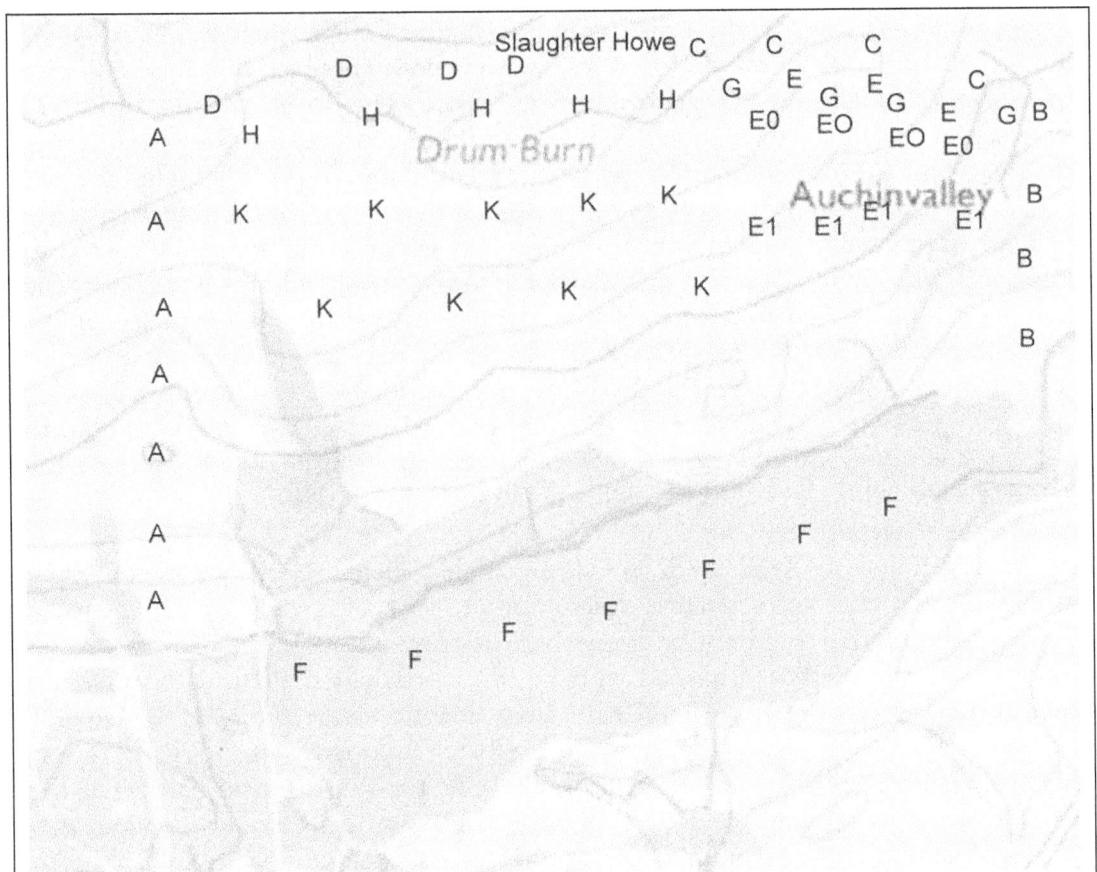

Map Data © 2018 Google (annotations, author) 55o59'16.04" N 4o01'27.08" W

Key
A = estimated Royalist start line
B = estimated Covenanter main line
C = Covenanter troop advance on hill
D = Royalist advance against Covenanter forces in the vicinity of the hill
E & E0 = Covenanter main advance of two regiments toward the foot of the hill and E1 = Hume's regiment unordered move toward the Royalist main line
F = Royalist infiltration up the Glen toward the Covenanter left flank
G = Earl of Crawford's cavalry support for Covenanter regiments on the right of the Covenanter line
H = Earl of Airlie's cavalry charge that routed Crawford's cavalry
K = Royalist main body charges against the Covenanter line, which, combined with Airlie's cavalry charge routed the Covenanter regiments

Figure 1. Map of the most plausible area that battle of Kilsyth took place.

It is not possible to determine the exact death toll on the Covenanter side, but a figure of 5,000-6,000 has been forwarded by Napier (c1838) .The source (SHS Volume 51-53, 1906) tells of up to 6,000 killed in the Covenanter army and only 6 or so (3 of which were Ogilvie's) in Montrose's royalist army. Such a low casualty figure on the Royalist side, if accurate, would throw serious questions on the assertions that Montrose's vanguard was close to collapse when saved from such a fate by the Earl of Airlie's cavalry. The source Napier (c1838) states only around 100 men of Montrose's army were "*hors de combat*", which would include seriously wounded, in its total (Napier, 1838). This slaughter of the Covenanter army was conducted not only on the field, but in a pursuit that the same source states covered 14 miles easterly from the battlefield.

There is no reliable way to determine if the Covenanter killed numbered as high as 5,000-6,000, however, it is clear that the toll was extremely high. For example, we know that most of the men formerly of Colonel Robert Cunningham's regiment (those that had not been killed at Alford) were killed at the battle of Kilsyth (Volume 18, GSC 1637-1651, 32, 1982). We are also informed by many non-primary sources that no quarter was given. However, an interesting letter document from Jean de Montereul to a Cardinal Mazarin, which makes the claim that up to 2,000 Covenanters were taken prisoner, reads 'The Earl of Holland has just come to tell me that Montrose has entirely defeated the Scottish army, and made 2000 prisoners' (SHS, Vol.29, Montereul Correspondence, Vol. 1, 1898). This figure seems high, but it has to be considered that some prisoners were taken, although this is conjecture that, to date, has not been proved or disproved.

Following the defeat of the Covenanter army at Kilsyth the Royalist army was able to March on Glasgow unopposed, the threat from this direction having evaporated. It is easy to think of Montrose's actions in the aftermath of the victory at Kilsyth as an opportunity lost for the Royalist cause as Montrose was in a position whereby he could have decided to stay in Scotland and move on Parliament in Perth to impose a government in the name of Charles I. This would have had the result of the Scottish Covenanter army in England having to return to Scotland to face the challenge. However, as defeat of the Covenanters and a subsequent advance into England to support the English Royalist's was the end-game of the campaign Montrose chose to advance southward and hasten battle with the Scottish Covenanter army returning North. This relieved him of the need to provide garrisons for strategic towns and further weaken his army. Despite not providing said garrisons, the cream of his Montrose's army, the redoubtable Gaels, had parted for home after the victory at Kilsyth, drastically weakening the Royalist army. This considered, moving South was to prove Montrose's undoing, the Royalist cause in Scotland, as it had in England, ending in disaster – Montrose, following defeat at Philiphaugh on 13 September 1645, effectively losing the Keys to Scotland that had been won at Kilsyth almost one month before.

POLITICAL REPERCUSSIONS

In actuality there was no need Montrose to move on Parliament following the victory at Kilsyth as parliamentary power was had lain with the Covenanter army in the shape of the Committee of Estates, which was, with the Covenanter army's destruction at Kilsyth, scattered and incapable of any coherent consultation (Volume 18, GSC 1637-1651, 1, 1982). In this respect, Montrose's victory at Kilsyth was not just another in a run of victories over the Covenanter armies, but effectively the toppling of the Scottish government. For a period of several weeks after that fateful day at Kilsyth, committee government in Scotland had completely ceased to function and to all intents and purposes did not exist all as the various members of the committee had not fled the field as a single body, but rather scattered in multiple directions (Volume 18, GSC 1637-1651, 1, 1982). This fact is explicitly recorded by the following text:

"For a month after Montrose's final victory at Kilsyth in August 1645 the covenanting administration virtually ceased to exist, and it was only re-established after forces from the Scottish army in England returned [from England] and routed Montrose at Philiphaugh in September [almost one Month after the battle at Kilsyth]" (Volume 18, GSC 1637-1651, XXVI, 1982).

Although there were instances of gatherings of "leading" covenanters at Duns on 26 August and Floors on 29 August, these, despite claims to the contrary, were not meetings of the Committee of Estates and had no real authority. A meeting held at Mordington on 3 September took on the role of communicating with the English Parliament (Volume 18, GSC 1637-1651, 2-3, 1982 & CSPD, 1645-7, 107-108), but it was not until after Montrose was defeated by the Scottish Covenanter army returned from England (this had returned to Scotland to confront Montrose's army) at Philiphaugh on 13 September 1645 that committee government really began to recover in Scotland. Although reliable records were not kept until around 16 October and formal record keeping did not recommence until the committee met at Glasgow on 21 October 1645, evidence shows that the Committee of Estates met somewhere near Stirling on 20 September (a week after Montrose was defeated at Philiphaugh), two meetings were held in Perth on 21 and 26 September respectively and further meetings were held at Duns in early October and at St Andrews on or around 14 October (Volume 18, GSC 1637-1651, 2, 1982 & HMC 8: 9th Report, 200). In this respect Montrose was the only true authority in Scotland between mid-August and mid-September 1645, despite not attempting to establish a parliament. While, as noted above, Montrose has been criticised for not marching on Parliament following his victory at Kilsyth, in reality the civil power base of the country had already been dismantled with the scattering of the Committee of Estates.

The defeat of Montrose at Philiphaugh just under one month after his victory at Kilsyth has directed the conventional historical view to suggest that Montrose's victory at Kilsyth had no real impact on the strategic direction of the wider civil war on both sides of the Anglo-Scottish border. In this respect the importance of the battle at Kilsyth has been overlooked in historiography. The battle has been treated as an anecdote lodged between the battles of Alford on 2 July 1645 and Montrose's defeat at the battle of Philiphaugh on 13 September 1645, which was devastating to the Royalist cause on both sides of the Anglo-Scottish border. However, such a view is fallacious as the immediate effect of the news of the Covenanter defeat at Kilsyth led to the Scottish Covenanter army fighting in England being ordered back to Scotland to face the threat from Montrose, with the aim of defeating same to restore Covenanter dominance in Scotland. It should be remembered that the Scottish Covenanter army, under the Earl of Leven, in England was laying siege to Hereford at the time news of Baillie's defeat at Kilsyth was received (SHS, Vol.29, Montereul Correspondence, Vol. 1, 1898). The decision to return North resulted in the siege being lifted on 1 September 1645. Therefore, Montrose's victory at Kilsyth had wide ranging effects on the war, denying the Scottish army in England victory at Hereford as the army marched North.[67]

It has to be considered that the defeat of Montrose at Philiphaugh was brought about by the severe depletion of his army. This had been brought about when several thousand highlanders – seasoned troops – had returned home after the victory at Kilsyth. This behaviour was the norm for highland clans, many of which fought for the plunder afforded them from their defeated enemy. Such plunder was bountiful from the captured Covenanter baggage train facilitating the conditions for departure from the army and Montrose's subsequent defeat at Philiphaugh the following month. Had Montrose's army achieved only a partial victory that had forced the Covenanters to take flight without suffering outright defeat then the Royalist army would have been fielded an additional several thousand seasoned troops stronger at Philiphaugh had Montrose still elected to march southward – such a strength would have vastly increased Montrose's possibility, even probability of victory. In this respect it was Montrose's victory at Kilsyth that facilitated the conditions that resulted in his defeat at Philiphaugh on September 1645.

END GAME

The defeats of the Royalist armies in England, the departure of highland clans from Montrose's army following the victory at Kilsyth and Montrose's subsequent defeat at Philiphaugh put the Royalist cause completely on the ropes, a situation that would end in acceptance of defeat with the surrender of the king, Charles I, to the Scottish Covenanter army at Newark in April 1646. This effectively put in place the mechanisms for ending the Civil War, which came to a close with the surrender of Royalist forces at Oxford on 24 June that year). Ironically, after helping the Parliamentarians to undisputed power in England, the inadequacy of the Scottish Covenanter Committee of Estates system, that had contributed to the Covenanter defeat at Kilsyth in 1645, would be a possible contributing factor that resulted in the Scottish defeat at Dunbar in 1650 (Volume 18, GSC 1637-1651, XIV, 1982) to an English Cromwellian army, an English occupation of Lowland Scotland following. Lowland areas yielded easily to English occupation, but some Highland clans, despite the preoccupation of some clans in renewed inter-clan warfare, provided an armed opposition, as was the case in the 1653 Glencairn rising, although general stability prevailed (Harris & MacDonald, 2007).

It can be considered that at Kilsyth, on 15 August 1645, Montrose[68] had won the

---

[67] The Royalist garrison at Herford surrendered later in the campaign

[68] Montrose (James Graham) was executed in Edinburgh on 21 May 1650. Less than three months later Scotland would be subjected to an English occupation through capitulation of the Covenanters at Dunbar

keys to Scotland when he defeated the Covenanter army and at Philiphaugh the following month the Covenanter victory effectively set in motion a chain of events that would lead to those keys being handed to England in 1650/51. The interregnum period of 1649-1660, which included the above mentioned English occupation of Lowland areas of Scotland, was followed by the Restoration with Charles II, a continuation of the Stewart Monarchy that would be coloured by many periods of unrest and open conflict leading up to, and including, the so called 'Glorious Revolution', of 1689 when Charles II's successor, James VI (Scotland)/James II (England), fled to France.

APPENDIX

Note 1: The source Napier, c1838 is clearly biased, and clearly bigoted in the assumption that breading made nobles more formidable in battle that a layperson. While this is known to be lamentably fallacious in the modern age, it is an unfortunate fact that non-nobles had it drummed into them from birth that they were inferior to noblemen that most, would have bested in combat in a different era

Note 2: It is claimed that many of the wives of the Irishmen and highlanders, as well as other women were captured and butchered in the forest at Methven (a few km to the west of Perth). If there is truth to this, then, assuming this news had reached Montrose's army, a better understanding may be presented for the mood that led to the slaughter of Covenanter troops fleeing the battle at Kilsyth.

BIBLIOGRAPHY

The History of Scottish Wars, From the Battle of the Grampian Hills, in the year 85, to that of Culloden, in the year 1746, 2nd addition, Edinburgh, 1825

Hogg, James, 1835 Tales of the Wars of Montrose Vol. II, , London, James Cochrane and Co, II Waterloo Place

Tales of the Wars of Montrose Voll.III, James Hogg, London James Cochrane and Co, II Waterloo Place 1835

Acts of Union 1707, Parliament

Baillie, Robert (David Laing), 1841-1842 The Letters and Journals of Robert Braille A.M., 1637-1662, Volume Second, Principal of the University of Glasgow, 2nd vol., Edited from the authors manuscripts, Edinburgh

The East Central Lowlands (Stirling, Falkirk & Kilsyth) – Maps of Scotland, Pont, Timothy 1560-1614, National Library of Scotland

Maps of Scotland, 1560-1928, National Library of Scotland

The North-part of England and the South-part of Scotland. Quartermaster's map, National Library of Scotland

Block 3 Open University module A200 Exploring History: medieval to modern 1400-1900, The Wars of the Three Kingdoms, 2nd Ed, 2001, The Open University, Milton Keynes

Montrose and the Covenanters, Their Characters and Conduct Volume II, Mark Napier

Harris, B & MacDonald, AR 2007 'Scotland, The Making and Unmaking of a Nation c.1100-1707', Volume 4: Readings, c.1500-1707, Dundee University Press and the Open University in Scotland

Erskine, C, MacDonald, AR and Michael Pennman 2007, 'Scotland, The Making and Unmaking of a Nation c.1100-1707', Volume 5: *Major Documents*, Dundee University Press and the Open University in Scotland

Harris, B & MacDonald, AR 2007 'Scotland, The Making and Unmaking of a Nation c.1100-1707', Volume 4, Volume 2:

Harris, B & MacDonald, AR 2007 'Scotland, The Making and Unmaking of a Nation c.1100-1707', Volume 2: *Early Modern Scotland: c.1500-1707*, Dundee University Press and the Open University in Scotland

Erskine, C, MacDonald, AR and Michael Pennman 2007, 'Scotland, The Making and Unmaking of a Nation c.1100-1707', Volume 5: *Major Documents*, Dundee University Press and the Open University in Scotland

Lynch M 2000 'James VI and the 'Highland Problem'' in Goodare, J. and Lynch M. (eds), *The Reign of James VI*, Tuckwell Press, Edinburgh

The source (Volume 51-53, 282 (340) is not impartial, in fact being downright disdainful of Covenanters.

Mosley, Charles, editor. Burke's Peerage, Baronetage & Knightage, 107th edition, 3 volumes. Wilmington, Delaware, U.S.A.: Burke's Peerage Ltd, 2003

Open University A200, Exploring History: Medieval to Modern 1400-1900, Block 3, The Wars of the Three Kingdoms

APS (Acts of Parliament Scotland), v, 268

APS (Acts of Parliament Scotland), v, 282-4

APS (Acts of Parliament Scotland), VI, I, 448

HMC 8: 9th Report, 200

Scottish History Society, 1982, Fourth Series, Volume 18, The Government of Scotland under the Covenanters 1637-1651, Printed for the Scottish History Society by Clark Constable Ltd, Edinburgh (1982)

P.A.12/I, minutes 16-31 October 1645; P.A.11/4, fos. 13IV-176V

CSPD, 1645-7, 107-108, Calendar of State Papers Domestic, Charles I (23 Vols., 1858-97)

Scottish History Society, Volume 51, Macfarlane's Geographical Collections relating to Scotland, 1906,

Scottish History Society, Volume 29 Montereul Correspondence, Volume 1, 1898

GLOSSARY

CSPD	Calendar of State Papers Domestic, Charles I (23 Vols., 1858-97)
ft	Unit of measurement
GSC	The Government of Scotland under the Covenanters
HMC	Historical Manuscripts Commission
km	Kilometre
m	Metre
PA	Parliamentary Records in the SRO
SHS	Scottish History Society
SRO	Scottish Records Office
±	Plus or minus

ABOUT THE AUTHOR

Hugh Harkins FRAS is a historian/physicist and author with a research background in astro/geophysics and studies/research in the wider scientific, aeronautic, astronautic and nautical technical and historical fields. He is also involved in research in the field of Scottish history, which formed a significant element of an otherwise scientific undergraduate degree. Hugh has published in excess of sixty books; non-fiction and fiction, writing under his given name as well as utilising several pseudonyms. He has also written for several international magazines, whilst his work has been used as reference for many other projects ranging from the aviation industry, international news corporations and film media to encyclopaedias, museum exhibits and the computer gaming industry. Hugh is a member of the Institute of Physics and is an elected Fellow of the Royal Astronomical Society. He currently resides in his native Scotland. Other titles by the author include:

Raid on the Forth – The First German Air Raid on Great Britain in World War II, 16 October 1939
Orbital/Fractional Orbit Bombardment System - The Soviet Globalnaya Raketa
Sukhoi T-4 Sotka – The Soviet Mach 3+ Hypersonic Missile Carrier/Airborne Reconnaissance System
Soviet Mixed Power Experimental Fighter Aircraft – Piston-Liquid Propellant Rocket Engine/Piston-Ramjet/Piston-Pulsejet & Piston-Compressor Jet Engine designs of the 1940's
Counter-Space Defence Co-Orbital Satellite Fighter
Into The Cauldron - The Lancaster MK.I Daylight Raid on Augsburg
Hurricane IIB Combat Log - 151 Wing RAF, North Russia 1941
RAF Meteor Jet Fighters in World War II, an Operational Log
Typhoon IA/B Combat Log - Operation Jubilee, August 1942
Defiant MK.I Combat Log - Fighter Command, May-September 1940
Blenheim MK.IF Combat Log - Fighter Command Day Fighter Sweeps/Night Interceptions, September 1939 - June 1940
Tomahawk I/II Combat Log - European Theatre, 1941-42
Fortress MK.I Combat Log - Bomber Command High Altitude Bombing Operations, July-September 1941
Air War over Syria, Tu-160, Tu-95MS & Tu-22M3 - Cruise Missile and Bombing Strikes on Syria, November 2015-February 2016
Light Battle Cruisers and the Second Battle of Heligoland Bight
British Battlecruisers of World War 1 - Operational Log, July 1914-June 1915
Iskander - Mobile Tactical Aero-Ballistic/Cruise Missile Complex
Sukhoi T-50/PAK FA - Russia's 5th Generation 'Stealth' Fighter
Sukhoi Su-35S 'Flanker' E - Russia's 4++ Generation Super-Manoeuvrability Fighter
Sukhoi Su-34 'Fullback'
Sukhoi Su-30MKK/MK2/M2 - Russo Kitashiy Striker from Amur
MiG-35/D 'Fulcrum' F – Towards the Fifth Generation
Sukhoi Su-27SM(3)/SKM
Russian/Soviet Aircraft Carrier & Carrier Aviation Design & Evolution Volume 1 - Seaplane Carriers, Project 71/72, Graf Zeppelin, Project 1123 ASW Cruiser & Project 1143-1143.4 Heavy Aircraft Carrying Cruiser
North American F-108 Rapier - Mach 3 Interceptor
Convair YB-60 - Fort Worth Overcast
Boeing X-36 Tailless Agility Flight Research Aircraft
X-32 - The Boeing Joint Strike Fighter

www.ingramcontent.com/pod-product-compliance
Lightning Source LLC
Chambersburg PA
CBHW080553030426
42337CB00024B/4854